FOR THE LOVE OF LIFE AND LAUGHTER

With A Few Tears Sprinkled In Between

MOTHER'S MEMOS- CHILDREN CHATTER-NATURES NUGGETS NUTTY NONSENSE

Marijayne

WESTBOW
PRESS°
A DIVISION OF THOMAS NELSON
& ZONDERVAN

WestBow Press books may be ordered through booksellers or by contacting:

WestBow Press
A Division of Thomas Nelson & Zondervan
1663 Liberty Drive
Bloomington, IN 47403
www.westbowpress.com
844-714-3454

ISBN: 978-1-6642-6292-8 (sc)
ISBN: 978-1-6642-6291-1 (e)

Print information available on the last page.

WestBow Press rev. date: 7/15/2022

I chose this as the main title with the thought that if we loved life enough to be able to laugh at ourselves, there would be fewer tears available to ruin our love of life.

~ Mary Schuttinga, author of *For The Love Of Life And Laughter With A Few Tears Sprinkled In Between*

. . . .

1ˢᵗ CORINTHIANS 16:4 NASB
Let all that you do be done in love.

Life at its Best

For the love of life and laughter.
The life we need to go after.
Pleasures we gain every day-
 laughter is smoothing the way.
Tears may be sprinkled in between-
our laughter and love of life.
There's so much more yet to be seen-
beyond the present day strife.

Ignore the tears you want to shed.
for nasty things somebody said.
When days are rough and hard to bear-
laugh at yourself - as if you don't care.
What is my reason for letting you know-
why I do think it's a good way to go?
What it the best for you to go after?
more love of life with a whole lot of laughter.

. . . .

1ˢᵗ Peter 3:10 NASB
Let him who means to love life, see good days.

Life—Is Whatever You Make it by God's Word

The sky may be dark and stormy - life's rain pours down on me-
God's Word is my umbrella - to protect and cover me.

When the road is rough and rocky - my walk may not be strong --
God's Word is my walking cane - to help me move along.

When the pace of life confuses me - and I don't know what to do
God's Word is my speedometer - slows me down to make it through.

I do have senior moments - whenever that may be-
Gods' Word helps me to remember- that He remembers me.

I may grow old and feeble - and will soon be going--going-- gone.
God's Word still does sustain me - as I pray and carry on.

. . . .

PSALM 119:11 NASB

Thy word have I have treasured in my heart that I may not sin against Thee.

Hold Fast on to your Dreams

Hold fast on to your dreams-
don't let them fade from view.
Don't let them wander elsewhere-
as dreams so often do.

Keep them ever in your mind-
Even closer to your heart.
Wipe the shadows from the window-
of your vision from the start.

Success is waiting for you-
Incredible though it seems-
You can make them all come true-
Just hold on to your dreams.

Hold fast on to your dreams-
the ones that made you strong.
Remember where you found them-
as it helped you move along.

In to it's joy you learned that life-
had much to offer you.
So hold fast on to your dreams
to make them all come true.

. . . .

1ˢᵗ Thessalonians 5:21 NASB
But examine everything carefully;
Hold fast to that which is good.

Walk with Me

Come along and walk with me
  Down life's road together.
We'll share each day completely-
  Through storms and sunny weather.
Keep my hand entwined with yours-
  To make each step seem lighter-
The love I see in your kind eyes-
  Will make the day much brighter.
And as our steps start slowing down-
  To catch each precious moment-
We'll know the days that hurried by-
  were days we so well spent.
And when those days fade into time-
  And will no longer be-
I'll know we shared the best of days -
  Because you came along and walked with me.

. . . .

1ˢᵗ JOHN 4:7a NASB
Beloved, let us love one another, for love is from God.

I Can Only Be Me

Love me for who I am-
  Not what you want me to be.
Over look my many faults-
  For I can only be me.
Look beneath the surface of my existance.
  Deep into what makes me who I am.
Listen- for I need someone to talk to.
  Don't shut me out-I need a friend.
Don't laugh at my foolish mistakes.
  Encourage me when I try to improve-
I want to be needed for myself
  and all your doubts remove.
I want to be needed for myself.
  for I truly can only be me.
Just love me for who I am.
  Not what you want me to be.

. . . .

ROMANS 15:7 NASB

Wherefore accept one another just as Christ also accepted us to the glory of God .

A Mans Sincere Proposal

Would you share a day with me-
a year or even life?
Could you bear to stay with me-
as my beloved wife?
Could I tell you dear one-
how much you mean to me?
Or would I so offend you-
your heart from me would flee?
Perhaps there is someone else
you're longing for each day -
If I'm the one you care for-
with you I'll always stay
But should you find I'm not the one
This is for me to say
I'll bother you no more dear one-
I'll just sadly go away.

. . . .

SONG OF SOLOMON 5:9 *a* NASB
What kind of beloved is your beloved, O most beautiful of women.

A Grooms Love for His Coming Bride

A golden halo of shimmering light,
surrounded her face of creamy velvet.
Her eyes were the color of ocean blue.
And I knew-Her cheeks were soft as the whisper of silk.
Her smile teased and sweetened her mouth,
glistened her lips like berries kissed by the morning dew.
And I knew- her soul was pure as wholesome milk.
Gentle breezes carried her body's perfume,
intoxicating me as she slowly came into view.
And I knew-for my heart beckoned her to come nearer.
She held out her hands to me-cool and tender.
Our eyes met and held a sweet promise to alway be true.
And I knew-there would never be anyone more dear.
Her finger slipped into the circle of gold
as our vows echoed the words of- I do.
And I knew-blessings were raining from heaven above.
Tenderly we embraced each other as one
and our kiss sealed the words of I love you.
And I knew-She would always be my Goddess of Love.

. . . .

SONG OF SOLOMON 4:1a NASB
How beautiful you are my darling.

The Bib Overall

He was tall and lanky with deep serious eyes.
    His smile came slowly-his chuckle a surprise.
His age didn't bother-he walked straight and tall-
    And was happiest wearing his bib overall.

His love for gardening was plainly shown.
    By all the veggies he yearly had grown.
He was seen in his garden from Spring until Fall-
    This stately man in a bib overall.

Now the hoe, rake, and shovel are idle and still.
    Though seeds he planted are growing at will.
Because the Master Gardner gave him a call-
    Saying Son, you'll no longer need your bib overall.

For I've readied a garment so clean and white-
    And a crown of jewels all glittery bright.
So enter my heaven of pure jasper walls-
    For you have done well in your bib overalls.

This Grandfather-Father-brother and friend-
    Did live a good life right to the end.
He left many memories for each to recall-
    The memories of a man in a bib overall.

. . . .

MATTHEW 5:8 NASB
Blessed are the pure in heart;
for they shall see God.

Make Believe Once Again

Beyond the years of make belief-
     A child stands in stately form of man.
With faded eyes and wrinkled brow-
     A shell remains that housed the child.
The hopes and dreams of make belief-
     Were turned aside by mans hurried days,
With toiling hands he hides desires -
     To make believe once again-to be a child.

Oh to be a child once again.
     without a worry or care.
To look at the sky as clouds float by.
     Wishing I could be there.
To fly like a bird to places unheard-
     So high on the wings of the wind-
Where wishes come true and dreams do too-
     and to be as a child once again.

. . . .

1ˢᵗ CORINTHIANS 13:11 NASB

When I was a child, I used to speak as a child, think as a child, reason as
a child. When I became a man I did away with childish things.

Front Porch Break

Remember the days which each house had a porch.
Out in front where folks took a break.
From all the toil and work of the day-
They'd rest there to sooth every ache.
Mom and Dad would sit quietly and visit a while-
In their rocking chairs placed side by side-
In the cool of the evening at the close of the day-
Watching their children with pride.
As they caught fireflies- to save in a jar-
And use shadows to play hide and seek.
Even the moon hid its face in a cloud-
For no one ever dared take a peak.
From the distant timber-echoing again and again-
Was the noise from the whippoorwill calls.
Crickets would join in the evening chorus-
Of The katydids song-as it rises and falls.
Sometime when you're weary and tired from life-
Stop a while for your sanity's sake-
In the cool of the evening- at the close of the day-
Take some time for a front porch break.

. . . .

MATTHEW 11:28 NASB

Come to Me all who are weary and heavy laden and I will give you rest.

Old Year-New Year

Where did the time go-so quickly it passed
        What did I do with it-that it went by so fast?
Each day so busy from daylight to setting sun-
        In no time at all -the day was soon done
The past year went by and before we knew.
        December arrived and it was soon through.
We have a new year before us today.
        Like an unwritten book with nothing to say.
It's pages are bare we have nothing to read.
        But we'll soon fill it up with a good or bad deed.
We never do know what each day will bring.
        We hope for happiness to make our heart sing.
Or it may be a heartache to bring spirits low-
        Where the year takes us we are destined to go.
Because all the days will soon hurry on-
        We'll again be surprised when this year is gone.
As we face a new year-and let go of the past.
        We'll wonder how long the memories wll last.
And when it is gone we'll question to know-
        We'll ask the same thing--where did the time go?

. . . .

PSALM 90:12 NASB

Teach us to number our days that we may present to thee a heart of wisdom.

The Progress of Time

When the sun came up this morning
      The day burst into light .
Quickly without warning-
      It soon became the night.
The moments, hours and many days-
      hurried into weeks.
Changing time in many ways-
      To months we did not seek.
As the months turned into years.
      So fast it made time flee-
Through laughter or with tears-
      We'll soon face eternity.
Where time won't really matter
      We wont need sunshine there.
Jesus will be the light that shines-
      For there will be-no night there.

. . . .

REVELATION 1:3 NASB

*Blessed is he who reads and those who hear the words of the prophecy
and heeds the things which are written in it for the time is near.*

Memories of Way Back When

As I remember Memorial day and loved ones from the past.
I won't forget the good times- that went by so very fast.
I'll bring flowers to their grave sight and gaze down at the sod-
As tears falls from my wrinkled face -I may even say, Why God?

Why did that precious son of mine--lose his life so young?
With only memories left behind-of a brave and loving son.
Yes, some die old and some die young-on life we can't depend.
While I am left to cry and hold-the memories of way back when.

Back when life felt secure-never thinking we would part-
Collecting all good memories-holding them close to my heart
Thank God for the precious memories-their goodness seem to last.
What takes the present hurt away? good memories of the past.

. . . .
REVELATION 21:4 NASB
And He shall wipe away every tear from their eyes; and there shall be no longer death; there shall be no longer any mourning, or crying, or pain, for the first things have passed away.

Advice to Myself

Don't cry for what might have been
   You chose this way to go!
With regrets I have to say-
   You know I told you so!
You knew it wouldn' t be all great-
   So here's the thing to do-
Forget the mistake of the past.
   Pick up yourself-start something new.

Go out and make your happiness.
   Reach out and find some fun-
Remember everyone has trials-
   You're not the only one
Smile at the world as it goes by.
   Bid farewell to the past.
Don't let your troubles get you down-
   You don't need them to last

. . . .

JUDE 1:2 NASB
May mercy, peace and love be multiplied to you

Do We Really?

We gripe about the weather.
　　　　We gripe about the war.
We stop to take a needed breath-
　　　　Then we gripe some more.
We gripe about the government.
　　　　We gripe to face the facts-
that we will do more griping-
　　　　When it's time for income tax.
We gripe about the preacher-
　　　　About the neighbors too-
No doubt there is someone-
　　　　Griping about me and you
We make a habit of griping-
　　　　Of that I have no doubt-
If we'd stop to count our blessings-
　　　　We'd have nothing to gripe about!

. . . .

PHILIPPIANS 2:14 NASB
Do all things without grumbling or disputing.

Don'ts and Do's

Don't say----"I wish" dreams would come true.
Do say ------"they will" by the things I do.

Don't say---"I hope" there's a chance for me.
Do say-------"I'll be" the best I can be.

Don't say---"I think" when unsure what to do.
Do say------"I know" and I'm positive too.

Don't say----"I wonder" why I don't rate.
Do say-------"With Gods help" I'll be something great!

Don't say----"I can't" before you even try.
Because if you do -your dreams will soon die.

. . . .

COLOSSIANS 3:17 NASB

*Whatever you say in word or deed do in in the name of the Lord
Jesus, giving thanks through Him to God the Father.*

The Worth of a Smile

When you are discouraged--you're efforts are in vane,
Who really wants to hear it--no need then to complain.
    Just smile---- and keep it to yourself.

When bound to lose your temper-as good folks so often do-
You want to wail and whimper-or swear a word or two.
    Just smile----and keep it to yourself.

So you've heard a bit of gossip-about a friend or foe.
Don't pass it on to someone else and tell them what you know.
    Just smile----and keep it to yourself.

Many times with just a smile--you'll make a better day.
You'll not be sorry all the while for things you didn't say.
    If you just smile and keep it to yourself.

. . . .
PSALMS 19:14 NASB
Let the words of my mouth and the meditation of my heart be
acceptable in Thy sight, O Lord my rock and my Redeemer.

When Shadows Grow

I hear his voice when all is still.
When from the past sweet thoughts reclaim.
The happy days ---then sadness fills my aching heart-
For he will not again speak my name.

Oh death where is your victory?
Your triumph has brought me low.
Yet memory will not let his voice be quiet-
I hear him when evening shadows grow.

His voice so clear I feel the nearness of him.
Almost a touch is felt upon my hand.
My love is gone but memories linger softly-
When shadows grow and stillness has command.

. . . .

JOB 17:7 LIVING BIBLE
My eyes are dim with weeping and I am but a shadow of my former self.

How Do You Say Goodbye?

How do you say goodbye to a friend?
  Who freshens your life like a soft summers wind.
Who captures your heart with her own special knack?
  With her warm smile that grows-til it buttons in back.
How do you say goodbye to a friend?

How do you tell her that she's loved a lot?
  For sharing herself with the talents shes got.
For patiently working 'til we understood-
  That we could unite in one sisterhood.
How do you say goodbye to a friend?

How do you tell her and not shed a tear?-
  Wanting so much- for her to stay here.
With the friends we hope- she'll never forget-
  I know this can't be-but I'm wondering yet-
How do you say goodbye to a friend?

. . . .

PROVERBS 17:17
A friend loves at all times.

A Little Late to Apologize

Turn back the time so I can change-
     The things I've done to cause you pain.
To make you want to go away-
     Turn back the time so I can say-
       I'm sorry.

And if I could only retrace the steps-
     To dry the tears that you have wept-
And calm the guilt I feel each day-
     Turn back the time so I can say -
       I'm sorry.

If years could turn around for me-
     If death were not reality-
I'd blot from time that cold sad day-
     Turn back the time so I can say-
       Dear friend-I'm sorry.

. . . .

PSALMS 34:13 NASB
Keep your tongue from evil and your lips from speaking deceit.

Moving Day

The van pulls away slowly and groans 'neath its load.
We will soon need to follow down a strange new road.

The house seems to beg me for its last good-bye.
As its empty rooms re-echo a sad and empty sigh.

I give the walls a loving touch, wipe a smudge from the floor-
Sadly gaze out the window and reflect the past once more.

Of the years when this old house was our safe dwelling place.
That sheltered our happy family -being blessed by Gods grace.

I caress the fireplace mantle with a gentle loving touch-
Remembering the many holidays-that we enjoyed so much.

The smell of many spices along with holly and pine-
Are etched in my memory with thoughts of a happy time.

My foot steps now sound hollow-as I walk to the door
Reminding me this very house will be for me no more.

But I have no time for sadness-I'll dry my tears and say
I had better keep on going---because ---today is moving day!

. . . .

PROVERBS 27:1 NASB

Do not boast about tomorrow for you do not know what a day may bring forth.

My Dad

He may not be a professer- or even a college grad.
But he has passed the test for me-because he is my Dad.

His hands are rough from labor, and sometimes he looks sad.
He sacrficed so much for me -because he is my Dad.

His steps are getting slower, he's lost some strength he had.
I don't mind -I love him still-because he is my Dad.

So often in a lifetime we'd change the things we had.
No need for me to change him-because he is my Dad

. . . .

EXODUS 20:12 NASB

Honor your Father and your Mother that your days may be
prolonged in the land which the Lord God gives you.

Mother's Memos

Mothers have the gift and talent for remembering what raising children is all about, trying to make good out of the mistakes they have made. Cherishing the happy moments that each child creates is priceless. Love of life and laughter is definitely a part of a mother's life along with some well earned tears.

BY MARIJAYNE

. . . .
JAMES 1:17 LIVING BIBLE
Whatever is good and perfect comes to us from God, the creator of all light and he shines forever without change or shadow, (verse 18) And it was a happy day for him when he gave us our new lives through the truth of his word and we became as it were, the first children in his new family.

New Born

Welcome little one- I've been waiting for you
*   For nine months I did- what all mothers do.*
Wanting to know- what you would be like-
*   Knowing you're perfect is such a delight.*
The waiting is over and its time to rest.
*   Sleep now as I hold you -close to my breast.*
As I marvel the fact- you're a part of me.
*   But who you look like-I just don't see-*
The resemblance will show I know before long-
*   But for now- little one-- Sleep on.*
Sleep on little one-as I'm watching you sleep.
*   As the years go by- this memory I'll keep.*
When just you and I were together alone
*   Getting acquainted about things unknown.*
Too soon I must share you with others who care-
*   For they have been waiting and they're not aware-*
That you did arrive just before dawn.
*   But for now- little one ---Sleep on*

. . . .

JAMES 1:4 NASB
Let endurance have its perfect result, that you may feel
perfect and complete, lacking nothing

Pretty Baby

Pretty baby -you dear little thing-
>
> So sweet so soft to the touch.

How can I tell the joy that you bring-
>
> and that I love you so much.

Your eyes so trusting as they look up at me.
>
> Your hand clasps my finger so tight.

Your smile too- is so precious to me-
>
> Pretty baby- you make everything right.

Even your tears tug at my heart.
>
> Your wet cheek next to my own.

Pretty baby- I've loved you right from the start-
>
> I'll love you long after you've grown.

I feel that I've known you ever so long.
>
> It seems that you've always been mine.

As I rock you and sing a lullaby song-
>
> The world all around me seems fine.

. . . .

1 JOHN 4:16a NASB

And we have come to know and have believed the love which God has for us.

Dream on Little One

Dream on little one- there's no worry or care.
As your mommy , I cherish the time that we share.
Little one- I must tell you- that I love you so.
But the dreams you dream -I may never know.
These fleeting momemts- very soon will be gone.
So for now - little one-dream on.

Dream on little one-you're so precious to me.
It's hard to believe- you are already three.
As I tuck you in- and see your sweet smile-
Enjoying your dream - for just a short while.
Sleep captured that smile and it was soon gone.
As you sleep- little one-dream on.

Dream on little one-as you rest in your bed.
You have so much of life -waiting ahead.
You may not remember-when you were just three.
When we were together- just you and me.
But I won't forget -this precious time when it's gone.
So good night little one- dream on.

. . . .

PROVERBS 3:24b NASB
when you lie down, your sleep will be sweet.

Little Shadow

You have a little shadow-
        that follows you each day.
Repeats every thing you do-
        and everything you say.
He tries to be just like you-
        and watches you each day-
All the good and all the bad-
        because he's taught that way.
Be watchful of your shadow-
        in what you make it do-
For he is your little copy -
        who tries to be like you.
Too soon he'll be a grown up-
        with ideas of his own.
You then will surely hear him say-
        I learned all at home!!!!

. . . .
PROVERBS 22:6 NASB
Train up a child in the way he should go. Even when he is old he will not depart from it

Naughty Night Mares

Mommy!-- came the frightened cry from a small voice down the hall.
  Mommy! I think I'm going to die, I can't get up at all!
My heart raced wild within me- as my feet went even faster-
  down the darkened hall to see-what caused this great disaster.
There upon the cold hard floor- lay my child beside his bed-
  I've never fallen so hard before-my small one tearfully said.
Gently I lifted my sleepy one and held him close to me-
  saying you are okay my son -no bruises do I see.

As I tucked the covers 'round him- I thought of future days.
  When he'd fall - because of sin -and be hurt in many ways.
As I put him back to bed I prayed- Lord hear him when he calls-
  And when the cleft of sin is high-Please catch him when he falls.
For I will not always be there -to lift him when he's down-
  He may be lying somewhere -upon the cold hard ground.
Though now he's just a little boy -when night mares frighten him-
  Please be there -when my grownup son- falls down because of sin.

. . . .
PSALMS 55:1 NASB
Give ear to my prayer O God: And do not hIde Thyself from my supplication.

Welcome to My Kitchen

You can come into my kitchen if you do not mind the mess!
It's where you'll see the biggest smiles from lots of happiness.

My kitchen is my favorite spot, its cheery warmth you'll feel--
I may not be the greatest cook-but you'll always find a meal.

Many feet come across my floor-some clean-some rather not!
But everyone is welcome here, I just keep a handy mop.

My house is often quite a mess, my kids have friends who meet.
But I enjoy their noisy fun, cause I know they're off the street.

Sometime if you should call on me and my dirt gives you stress-
Feel welcome just to grab the mop and help clean up the mess!

. . . .

HEBREWS 13:2 NASB
Do not neglect to show hospitality to strangers, for by this,
some have entertained angels without knowing it.

Why O Why am I so Lucky?

While others suffer in this world with war on every hand-
With hatred bringing death unfurled to meet sins great demand-
                                        Why am I so lucky?
Their children dying in the cold while mine are warm and fed.
Suffering many things untold among their naked dead-
                                        Why am I so lucky?
Am I better in God'd eyes- or has my soul more worth?
Am I favored as a prize- because of nobler birth? No?
                                        Then why am I so lucky?
I do not know why in my life -I'm blest the way I am.
While others suffer war and strife - in many a ruined land-
                                        Why O why am I so lucky?

. . . .
MATTHEW 24:6 NASB
And you will be hearing of wars and rumors of wars. See that you do not be frightened, For these things must take place, but that is not yet the end.

Todays Birthday Girl

Today ---your baby shoes were put away.
    Little girl, you grew up way too fast.
Today---I bowed my head to pray-
    for the hope your childhood joys will last.

Today ---we'll add another year-
    with the candle on the cake for you.
Today--- I brushed away a tear-
    And a wish that all your dreams come true.

Today--- may God's wisdom light the day-
    with an angel to guide in all that you do.
As you meet each challenge along the way -
    May He always be watching over you.

. . . .

ISAIAH 58:11a NASB
And the Lord will continually guide you.

Mom's Darling Daughter

What makes the sunshine dim in space?
Who touches your heart with love and grace?
Who brings a smile to a mother's face? A daughter---a darling daughter.
Who's a tiny image of ones self?
A perfect picture of life and health-
A treasure you love more than wealth- -- A daughter---a darling daughter.
Who keeps you always on your toes?
Buying scads of shoes with unmatched clothes-
Whose mood changes as fashion goes- --A daughter-a darling daughter.
Who makes you sometimes want to scream?
When her messy room is never clean-
And often thinks you're very mean----A daughter--a darling daughter.
Who warms your heart at the end of the day?
With her goodnight kiss as you hear her say-
I love you Mom-you're doing okay-- A daughter---a darling daughter.

. . . .

PROVERBS 31:29 NASB
Many daughters have done nobly, but you excel them all.

Moms Wedding Wishes

Dear daughter will you stop a while - on your very busy day.
  And listen to your mother now- of what I have to say.
You have a very special place-in my heart and in my life-
  It's hard now to realize-soon you too will be a wife.
Your birth was such a nice surprise as I held you close to me-
  A girl they said- and one so sweet -as you were meant to be.
Seems yesterday you came to me-with shoe strings to be tied-
  The little scratch upon your hand -I kissed it when you cried.

I watched you walk away to school-so proud-no fear of harm
  Your little feet when er' so fast from my protecting arm.
The years slipped by much too fast-in your teens I loved you more.
  We shared one another's dreams and laughter by the score.
And now in all your happiness-a tear I'll wipe away-
  I shall not cry much when you leave- this is your special day.
I pray that in your marriage - your home God will bless-
  With a little girl as sweet as you-to bring the same happiness.

. . . .

PROVERBS 12:4 NASB
An excellent wife is the crown of her husband.

Grown Up Little Boy

You'll always be my little boy-though you are now a man.
And soon to be a husband with a future in the plan.

As you begin your marriage- with a girl so sweet and fine-
Love her much because I feel- she'll be like a daughter of mine.

It makes me feel a little sad - how fast the years did go-
But those days of the past-gave me time to watch you grow.

You'll need a guide through married life- let God be the one.
To keep you faithful to your wife-as soon as it's begun.

Through all the days that hurried by- you've been a source of joy
From many things remembered, and you'll always be my little boy.

. . . .

PROVERBS 6:20 NASB
My son, observe the commandments of your Father and
do not forsake the teaching of your Mother.

Mother in Law

Soon my son will marry
*   to the girl of his choice.*
May I show my love for her-
*   in deed as well as voice.*
Let me look upon her-
*   as if she were my own.*
As though she lived here always-
*   in the comfort of my home.*
Help me not to criticize-
*   though different she may be.*
My way will be strange to her-
*   as hers will be strange to me.*
It doesn't matter if she calls me-
*   Mother-Mom- or Ma-*
I pray she'll never need to say-
*   I'm a meddling Mother-in Law.*

. . . .

PROVERBS 21:23 LIVING BIBLE
Keep your mouth closed and you'll stay out of trouble

Gone But Not Forgotton

Empty arms-that ache to hold him.
A broken heart -that failed to mend.
My whole life -came crashing down-
When my baby's life -came to an end.

Deep valleys I struggled to walk through.
Mountains of grief -were so very high.
Nothing I did -healed the pain in my heart.
As over and over- I asked the Lord --Why?

With patience He tenderly told me.
Holding me close as I cried.
Reminding me-He does understand.
For He too-had a Son that died.

He died because of His love for us.
And He opened my eyes to see.
My sweet baby-cradled in His strong arms.
Healing my heart and comforting me.

. . . .
2nd CORINTHIANS 1:3
Blessed be the God and Father of our Lord Jesus Christ,
the father of mercies and God of all comfort.

Children's Chatter

BY MARIJAYNE

Children's Chatter brings clarity to the love of laughter.
Who doesn't love to hear the chatter and laughter of children?
You are blest if you have listened to their chatter and laughed
happy tears.

. . . .

Proverbs 31:28a NASB
Her children will rise up and bless her

As Seen Through the Eyes of a Child

There is nothing to be compared to the wonder of things seen
through the eyes of a child. The imaginations of a young mind
brings freshness to things common and taken for granted by
those considered to be wiser. Also to listen to their chatter
even while talking to themselves, is a joy that a mother wants
to treasure and deposit in her memory bank.
With much joy and a little sadness, I have tried to capture on the
following pages, moments from my own childhood as well as
from my children.

. . . .

PROVERBS 21:11

Even a child is known by his doings whether his work is pure and whether it is right.

Daddy's Hand

I could climb a mountain
       Or cross the Canyon Grand.
Or sail the mighty ocean-
       If Daddy held my hand.

I could go to Africa.
       Or some other distant land-
I'd be as brave as I could be-
       If Daddy held my hand.

When Daddy holds my hand-
       most ten feet tall I stand.
I'm not afraid of anything-
       when Daddy holds my hand.

. . . .

PROVERBS 10:1 NASB
A wise son makes a Father glad.

If I Could

If I were but a tiny thing
        as small as I could get-
I'd walk among the raindrops
        and never feel the wet.

If smaller than a whisper
        of a summer wind that's hot-
I could hide behind a shadow
        and pretend that I an not!

Small as a broken bubble
        smaller than a tiny dot-
Like the hole within a doughnut
        I am there and yet I'm not!

What fun I would have with you-
        the places I could go-
Riding high upon your shoulders
        and you would never know.

I could do so many things
        and I would be all set-
If I were but a tiny thing
        as small as I could get.

. . . .

PROVERBS 20:11 NASB
It is by his deeds that a lad distinguishes himself.

Naughty Playmate

A rattle at the window. A tapping at the door.
Listen to that naughty wind blowing more and more.
Begging me to play outside - but really don't you see-
I'm afraid I'll start to cry-the way it teases me.

It blows hard into my face. then tossles my hair about.
Such a naughty playmate, so why should I go out?
Yesterday it blew my cap - over the garden wall.
It took it most a mile away, I have none to wear at all!

It laughed when I climbed the wall, to see where it had blown-
I watched it travel out of sight, like a bird it has flown.
I'm asking you naughty playmate, "Go and find my cap."
And bring it gently back to me -while I go take a nap.

. . . .

PSALMS 4:8a NASB
In peace I will lie down and sleep .

Back Yard Sand Pile

I have a very special land. Where toes sink deep and feel so grand.
And castles grow the way I plan, from out of tiny grains of sand.
I like to play there all the while- In my back yard sand pile.

Tunnels hollowed deep inside-So cool where kittens like to hide.
Behind a stick fence safely tied-To keep them safe I must decide.
To dig more sand with a smile- In my back yard sand pile.

All the roads are patted hard- along the fence of each new yard.
I told my dog to stay on guard. To keep it all from getting marred.
I want to keep it fresh in style-In my back yard sand pile.

Will you come and play with me? You'll find me under an old oak tree.
My roads and castles you will see- that's where I will most often be.
Enjoying each day all the while. In my back yard sand pile

. . . .
PSALM 127:3 LIVING BIBLE
Children are a gift from God. They are his reward.

Castle Dreams

If I could build a castle upon a fluffy cloud-
      I'd softly walk through my yard
And I would be so proud.
      To have my castle move along-
And float into your view-
      So you could see me playing there-
Smiling down at you.

There's steps up to my castle.
      It takes a dream like mine.
To climb up to this special place-
      where every thing is fine.
Come dream with me in cloud land-
      I'll be waiting for you there.
We'll sail along together-
      And go traveling everywhere.

. . . .

GALATIANS 4:20 LIVING BIBLE

How I wish I could be there with you right now, and not have to reason
with you like this for at this distance I frankly don't know what to do.

The End of a String

If I could fly- away up on high-
     Like a kite on the end of a string
Up to the sky-away up on high-
     It would be the most wonderful thing.
Up to the clouds -where birds fly by-
     And with every flap of their wing-
They'd wonder why- this strange bird-
     Was tied on the end of a string.
Flipping and flopping-bouncing around.
     Hearing the wind whistle and sing-
As it carries me away-further on high-
     Safely tied on the end of a string
Some time when I fly -up in the sky
     On a beautiful day in the Spring.
I may fly away- far out of your sight-
     Like a kite on the end of a string.

. . . .

PROVERBS 23:5c

Like an eagle that flies toward the heavens.

Children's-Cart Wheels

With a hippity hop and a flippity flop-
  And a summer-salt right over the top.
Then a jumpity jump on to a stump-
  Landing their feet with a bumpity bump.
Away they will go with a skippity skip-
  For one more time to flippity flip.
Into the air with legs ziggity zaging-
  Back and forth they go jiggity jagging.
Though their sweat goes drippity drop.
  They still continue to hippity hop.
Clapping their heels with a clicky clack-
  Over again from front to back
Children at play in a world all their own-
  Can make believe that is well known.
As they hippity hop and flippity flop-
  Again and again right over the top.

. . . .

JAMES 1:4 NASB
Let endurance have its perfect result, that you may be
perfect and complete, lacking in nothing.

Daddy-May I

May I help you Daddy? said a little boy one day.
Sure-You can be my helper, if you do it all my way.
But Daddy, I'm too little, to follow your big plan-
Bring it down to my size, and I'll do the best I can!
Son, My plan was never made - for little boys to do.
So get along somewhere else -I haven't time for you!
I've got to get this job done - before the sun goes down.
Find something else to do- Just don't hang around!

May I help you, my Son --his Daddy said one day
Sure -you can be my helper- if you do it all my way.
But Son, I'm too old - to follow your big plan-
Change it into my size- then I'll do the best I can.
Dad- my plan was never made- for older men like you!
Get along somewhere else --find something else to do.
Too late Dad remembered - words that make him sad.
His little boy had now become- to be just like his Dad.

. . . .
PROVERBS 3:13 NASB

How blessed is the man who gains wisdom and the man who gains understanding,

Magic Moments

There's magic in a friendly smile
       of dear ones when they meet.
The magic of a mother's love
       is something extra sweet.
The magic of a hand clasp
       of friends that happen by.
The magic of a tear drop
       in a pretty maidens eye.
Magic of laughter above the noise
       of a busy crowd you see-
Gives comfort to a lonely heart
       wherever you may be.
Magic moments give us joy
       but the best you ever saw
Is when a small child says to you -
       I do love you, Grandma.

. . . .

PSALMS 128:5 LIVING BIBLE
*May the Lord continually bless you with heavens blessings as well as
with human joys. May you live to enjoy your grandchildren.*

Natures Nuggets

BY MARIJAYNE

The beauty of life and nature is seen by every eye that looks for it, in spite of the storms that may come to destroy it, God helps nature find a way to heal the damage and make it beautiful again, bringing back the joy of love and laughter.

. . . .

1 JOHN 1:4 NASB
And these things we write, so that our joy may be complete.

Spring Rain

Raindrops tap my windows.
            gentle, hushed and still.
Telling me of coming rain-
            sweeping down the hill.

Darkened skies above me-
            scowling with dispair.
Rolling clouds and lofty winds-
            pushing here and there.

Soon the drench is over.
            The sun begins to shine.
The birds resume their singing-
            The world looks clean and fine.

And over in the meadow
            the snow was dirty grey-
So quickly now the spring rain-
            has washed winter away.

. . . .

HEBREWS 6:7a NASB
For the ground that drinks
the rain which often falls upon it, and brings forth
vegetation useful to those whose sake it is also tilled
receives blessings from God

Unpredictible

Spring has sprung, it's just begun.
To make the grasses greener.
It's good to know the dirty snow-
Will change to something cleaner.

Showers bring May flowers.
A fact most everyone knows.
But half the time the sun will shine-
Or it snows amd snows and snows.

Then the sprouts will have to wait.
To come above the ground.
No doubt- they will not appear-
Until Springtime settles down.

. . . .

SONG OF SOLOMON 2:11,12a LIVING BIBLE
The winter is past. The rain is over and gone. The flowers are springing
up and the time of singing birds have come. Yes, Spring is here .

Summer Evening

In the warmth of a summer evening- when crickets harmonize-
And the full moon creates shadows-as it brightens up the skies.
The wind gently moves the clouds-to encourage the coming rain-
And the daisies nod a welcome- to the raindrops for the gain.
As the summer eve continues -I'm challenged to stay and sit.
I wrap my coat around me -for the air cooled quite a bit.

I'm sheltered with my umbrella- I brought for my protection.
But the raindrops keep on coming- from every other direction.
By now- there's quite a chilling wind-to convince me to decide-
To enjoy his summer evening-I had better go inside.
Now I'm looking out the window-and I can't see a single thing.
This dark summer evening is behaving just like spring.

. . . .

ECCLESIASTES 7:13 LIVING BIBLE

See the way God does things and fall in line.---- Don't fight the facts of nature.

Autumn Wind

Tumbleweeds roll ahead of its breath-
*   to be caught by the corner fence.*
It flirts with a whistle to a dancing sunbeam-
*   as she pauses in fearful suspense.*

Leaves that were raked in a neat little pile-
*   are huddled to keep on their guard-*
Hear the wind laugh as it stirs them about-
*   and sweeps them around on the yard.*

It tortures the willow 'til it weeps to the ground-
*   then hurries to catch a loose cap-*
To sail it away where it can not be found-
*   and makes us hold tight to our wrap.*

Skies are blown clear of scurrying clouds-
*   The night eerie as it howls all the more.*
The luminous moon calmly looks down-
*   as the wind continues to roar.*

Slowly it blows itself out of breath-
*   each quieter than the one before*
It sighs with a whisper and seems quite content-
*   to rest 'til it knocks on next mornings door.*

. . . .

JOHN 3:8 NASB
The wind blows where it wishes and
you hear the sound of it, but do not know where it comes
from and where it is going.

The Passing of Autumn

Lacy patterned cobwebs covered with morning frost-
Was the Bridal veil for Autumns breath taking beauty.
 As she walked down the isle of warm days
Into the waiting arms of Winter.
Gentle at first was Winters love for her-
Showering his bride with snow flakes of kindness.
Only to reveal his cold heart in future days-
as the grasp of his icy fingers, smothered the life
from my beautiful Autumn.
Though she now lies still and cold-buried beneath
a blanket of frozen nature, her memory lingers
with all those who loved her rare beauty.
Remembered In the heart of all those
who shared happiness with her.
But soon forgotten when Spring brings a new love
Of warm days, green grass, sunshine and flowers.

. . . .

JAMES 1:24 NASB
*For once he looked at himself and gone away he has immediately
forgotten what kind of a person he was.*

Falling Leaves and Time

Each golden leaf that tumbles down;
*   upon the newly frozen ground.*
Is like the days once fresh and bright-
*   that quietly fades into the night.*
The leaves and days- each holding fast-
*   must lose itself when time is past.*
Without a hope to grasp again-
*   as leaves the fading day must end.*
Each fragile leaf with beauty bold-
*   reflects the day when turning gold-*
Will cling until time says--no more-
*   to drift like leaves and days before.*
Each golden leaf each lovely day-
*   must in its time give self away.*
So future days and leaves in Spring-
*   can take their place on passing wing.*

. . . .

PSALMS 4:12 NASB

So teach us to number are days that we may present to thee a heart of wisdom .

Seasons First Snow

Dainty snowflakes pause in mid-air---debating
      Whether to commit themselves to earth or space.
A timid sun peaks out with cautious care –
      then promptly pulls the clouds across its face.
The air is hushed as each flake tumbles down.
      Catching one another in their play.
Children look up to feel the cool touch
      of each flake in their moment to stay.
The warm earth stretches to welcome the snow
      It clings fast -dismissing its fears-
It caresses the ground then soon melts away-
      To lose itself among visible tears.
The wind dies down but only to pause-
      Then returns as if no time to waste-
To cover the scars of the brown blemished earth-
      It carries more snow in its haste.
Wet and woolly the flakes flurry down-
      With happy heart I watch them fall to earth.
The stinging wind brings extended labor-
      The first of snows is joyfully giving birth.

. . . .

PSALMS 45:1a LIVING BIBLE
My heart is over flowing with a beautiful thought.

Wishing on a Star

Come out O star that I may wish-
      Upon your light that shines.
Into my heart where wishes grow-
      Where life and hope entwines.
Come out O star that I may see-
      Your brilliance in the night.
So I can hope for better things-
      And wish that wrongs get right.
Come out O star that I may know-
      when night fades into day-
You'll come again when night time falls-
      to shine and light the way.
Come out O star that I may have-
      A guide to wish upon-
Though dark the night -you're guiding light
      Will shine until the dawn.

. . . .

1 CORINTHIANS 15:41 LIVING BIBLE
The sun has one kind of glory. While the moon and stars have another kind,
and stars different from each other in the beauty and brightness

The Forgotten Tree

The laughters gone I stand alone-
      Without my lights and tinsel.
Among the piles of paper stuff-
      I feel naked as a pencil.

I was so grand in splendor.
      Bright gifts beneath my bough
I now am stripped of everything-
      Christmas time is over now.

My boughs are drooped in sadness.
      They have all forsaken me.
They'll soon forget I ever was-
      Their family Christmas tree.

. . . .

PSALM 31:12 NASB
I am forgotten as a dead man, out of mind.

The Odd Couple

Father Time and Mother Nature- a couple you can't control.
They've been together forever-Since God created them whole.

Father Time has his moments- he keeps busy by the hour.
He never wastes time away-as it's directed by Gods power.

Mother Nature arranges seasons. All four she mothers along.
Changeable as the weather-Sometimes right-sometimes wrong!

Most of the time they do okay-whether to be or not to be--
But it gets a little stormy when they agree -to disagree.

. . . .
GENESIS 8:22 NASB
While the earth remains, seed time and harvest,
cold and heat, summer and winter, day and night shall not cease.

Winter Artist

Jack Frost with his big long nose -and icicles on his chin.
Swinging along his brush with paint- Smiling a frosty grin.

Silently- he fashions his work -as he travels everywhere.
Flocking the branches of naked trees -with beauty beyond compare.

Finishing his work before the dawn-he empties his paint and brush-
Spreading frost on my windows - then goes off with a rush.

When the morning sun begins to shine- to my great surprise-
The picture on my window- is a frosty white sunrise.

. . . .
GENESIS 31:40 NASB
Thus it was by day- the heat consumes me and the frost by night. That which has
been done is that which will be done, so there is nothing new under the sun.

Nutty Nonsense

BY MARIJAYNE

If you don't enjoy nutty nonsense, you're missing something given to you that may remove stress in your life. I believe there is a healing process within us that helps us enjoy a bit of nutty nonsense and preserves our health with the love of life and laughter. God gave us the ability to laugh and the Bible says in

Proverbs 17:22 NASB
A joyful heart is good medicine.

Reflections of a Country Girl

When I was a little girl-
  living on the farm.
I couldn't claim much beauty-
  nor very little charm.
My hair was straight as Grandma's broom-
  tiny freckles on my nose-
My dress was long -then too long short-
  because---I wore hand me down clothes.
Pastime was just climbing trees-
  catching frogs in a muddy ditch-
Swinging on a wild grape vine-
  like a merry flying witch.
I reckon when they made this girl-
  they forgot the sugar and spice.
So aren't you really quite surprised-
  that I grew up to be so nice?

. . . .

PSALMS 139:14a LIVING BIBLE
Thank you for making me so wonderfully complex ! It is amazing to think about.

Birth of a Poem

While laboring to put my thoughts into verse-
  With all it's pleasures -some times its a curse.
For when I try hard the right word to get-
  To give the thought meaning I strain and I sweat.
My forced inspiration is bitter as gall-
  when the battered sentence has no rhyme at all.
I fight for control and don't even yell-
  So when labor has ended-no one can tell-
The birth pains I had while travailing in verse-
  Was almost the death of me or even much worse.
I could have aborted the whole sorry mess-
  And give in to the feelings of pity and stress.
I could have dismissed this brain child of mine-
  It made my soul struggle from the very first line.
But I would never have known-had I sought to destroy.
  The birth of a poem --with its satisfying joy.

. . . .

1 JOHN 1:4 NASB
And these things we write so that our joy will be complete.

Me and Myself

I can never explain the way of myself.
The secrets that only I know.
That innermost self is alway there-
and stays with me wherever I go.

Agreeing with others I usually do-
As for seeing myself eye to eye-
Far harder it is when I'm faced with a task
to agree with myself-though I try.

Friends are ignored when we don't agree-
along with the enemies I know.
But that miserable me does not go away-
I have me wherever I go!

Now if me or myself were somebody else.
I know, I could see what was wrong
Far easier it is to see their mistakes-
and know where corrections belong.

But when I look happy and wear a big smile.
Like the smile on the face of an elf-
You can be sure we're doing okay-
And I'm getting along with myself.

. . . .
1ST CORINTHIANS 4:4 NASB
*I am conscious of nothing against myself, yet I am not by this
acquitted; but the one who examines me is the Lord.*

Is It Really Like That?

Days come and days go- where they come from-I don't know.
Though they go in many ways- they soon become our yesterdays.

What goes around -comes around-of this I have no doubt.
Sometimes it's hard to understand- what that is all about!

What we sow is what we reap-You can not change the fact.
If we don't reap what we sow- we won't survive -on what we lack.

Life's road will lead to somewhere-no matter which way we go-
We may get lost and forget -where we've been- we'll never know.

This poem may seem-out of this world-and spacey in every way-
If it doesn't make any sense to you-just dump it into yesterday.

. . . .

PSALM 90:4 NASB

For a thousand years in Thy sight are like yesterdays when it passes by.

Just too Busy

Busy in the neighborhood -busy in the church
Busy being busy-busy in the search.
For things to keep me busy, so I can earn a dime
*Busy in a hurry so I can die **on time**.*

I would call this nutty nonsense- not even worth a laugh-
And since I've thought it over- I must find a better path.

If I keep on being busy - working harder every day.
I will age a lot faster-growing old and turning gray,

I have a choice of what to do-To make my life sublime
*If I don't change my busy days- I 'll die- **before my time***

. . . .
ECCLESIASTES 7:17 *b* NASB
Do not be a fool! Why should you die before your time?

Single Guys Beware

MY guy's got to have character-dark brown eyes and lots of dough.
Tall and lanky and very smart-not too fast and not too slow.
He's got to have a mouth that grins-with teeth so white and fine.
He's got to show me off in style.-when he takes me out to dine.
He better not be cross eyed---pigeoned toed or flat-
In his pockets or in his head ---for I'll take care of that.
He's got to have a limousine and a figure that's streamlined.
He better not have flat feet---or they would match with mine.

First of all I'm going to say- I guess he better be-
In love in the one he marries - and frankly I mean me!
He better not look at another-for I would squash him flat.
He really wouldn't be much good-in a shape as bad as that!
He has to be sure to get a maid -and be at every meal-
And when some day I find him ---he'll know that I am real!

. . . .
PROVERBS 21:19 LIVING BIBLE
It is better to live in a desert land than with a contentious and vexing women.

If and Maybe

IF and **MAYBE** met one day- in the middle of a decision.
Neither could make up their mind-which led to a devision.
MAYBE *should and* **IF** *should not-they just could not agree.*
On why the other wanted it to be or not to be.
You're so confused said **MAYBE,** *you can't make up your mind!*
Do you suppose you'll always be, the undecided kind ?
Well said **IF**-*I'm not so sure-you're better now than me.*
Why were you the chosen one to have the name of **MAYBE?**
And why am I just a tiny **IF** - *I can not seem to grow.*
And why do we agree to disagree? I guess we'll never ever know!

. . . .
ECCLESIASTES 4:9 LIVING BIBLE
*Two can accomplish more than twice as much
as one, for the results can be much better.*

Grandma Used to Say

A lid for every kettle-
     and soup for every dish.
My Grandma used to say to me-
     whenever I would wish.
That someone like Prince Charming-
     would sweep me off my feet.
We'd live happy ever after-
     and life would be complete.
Now -Grandma meant there's someone-
     for everyone in life.
A girl for every husband-
     and a man for every wife.
But what really concerns me
     in spite of what I wish-
That the lid won't find its kettle-
     and the soup won't find its dish.

. . . .

PROVERBS 18:22 LIVING BIBLE
The man who finds a wife finds a good thing; She is a blessing to him from the Lord.

Just an Old Grouch

Growing old is so unfair.
      The past is past- the future is where?
There are aches in places- I forgot I had-
      Former happiness only makes me sad.
My bones report a change in the weather.
      And I try not-- to trip over a feather.
Teeth and hair have turned to gray-
      I can't remember what I want to say.
Hearing aides to hear---Bifocals for to see-
      Yes, growing old seems unfair to me.
The golden years have lost their shine.
      If you don't like yours-you can have mine.

. . . .

PSALMS 144: 3,4 LIVING BIBLE

O Lord, what is man that you even notice him?
Why bother with the human race? For man is
but a breath; his days are like a passing shadow.

In Case You Haven't Noticed

I'm growing old -it's in my bones-
    They refuse to bend to my will.
What's more my eyes are strained to see-
    The directIons to take this new pill.
Each day I find a new wrinkle-
    and more and more gray in my hair.
I'm much too cold in the summer-
    to part with my long underwear.
My ears can't bear small noisy children-
    Though TV --I turn up full blast!-
Grandma -- lived to be ninety
    I doubt very much if I'll last.

. . . .

PSALMS 38:9a LIVING BIBLE
Lord, You know how I long for my health once more.

Old Mans Complaint

When I was young- I could spit a mile.
      Now it barely goes beyond my smile.
I could run and jump without a care-
      Now I have to hold onto a chair,
I had hair so thick I could barely comb.
      All I have now is a shiny dome.
My skin was soft-my cheeks were pink.
      Teeth so white that didn't stink.
My complexion now is rough and pale.
      I soak my teeth but to no avail.
They still need help because I swear-
      They smell as bad as my underwear!
But I can't complain-for I'll soon forget.
      My memory is not the same--and yet-
If I keep it quiet and my age not told-
      They may not notice that I'm growing old.

. . . .

PSALMS 71:9 LIVING BIBLE

And now, in my old age, don't set me aside. Don't forsake me when my strength is failing.

My Pity Party

Today I am having a pity party-
*   I tried to invite everyone.*
But to my hurt they told me-
*   they didn't want to come.*

I tried to explain the reason-
*   when they rejected me-*
They didn't want to listen-
*   to my sad and desperate plea.*

They didn't really care at all-
*   that I'm here all alone.*
Why?--because they were also having
*   a pity party of their own!*

. . . .
HEBREWS 4:16 NASB
Let us therefore draw near with confidence to the throne of grace that we
may receive mercy and may find grace to help in the time of need.

Printed in the United States
by Baker & Taylor Publisher Services